Table of Contents

What Are Dolphins?

Dolphins are mammals that are members of the toothed whales family. Other members of this family are orcas and beluga whales.

There are 43 different kinds of dolphins. They differ in where they live, size, and coloration.

Size

The smallest kind of dolphin is the Maui's dolphin. It can grow to be about four feet in length and weigh about ninety pounds.

The largest kind of dolphin is the orca. They can grow to be about 25 feet long and weigh over 16,000 pounds.

The bottlenose dolphin can be up to twelve feet long. They can weigh over 400 pounds.

Physical Characteristics

Dolphins have a powerful tail fin, which is called a fluke. Their body is smooth and rounded. These features help them to swim fast.

Dolphins are usually gray, black, and white. They may have spots or other markings on their body.

Dolphins have a blowhole on top of their body. They use this to breathe when they come to the surface.

Habitat

Most dolphins live in the tropical areas of the ocean, where the water is warm. Some are found close to the **coast**, others are found in the open ocean.

Some dolphins, like the Amazon river dolphin, are able to live in rivers.

Range

Dolphins are found around parts of every continent except Antarctica.

Dolphins are often seen off the coast of Portugal, New Zealand, the Bahamas, and Hawaii.

Diet

Dolphins are **carnivores**. They eat only meat.

Their diet is made up of mostly fish and squid. Dolphins that are closer to the coast may also eat **crustaceans**.

Many dolphins do not chew their food. They swallow it whole or break smaller pieces off.

Some kinds of dolphins work together to hunt for food.

A few dolphins herd the fish into a small area and keep them there. The rest of the dolphins swim through the fish to catch and eat them. They switch places so that they all get a chance to eat.

Orcas are a kind of dolphin.

They often work together to

hunt for food.

Communication

Dolphins use sound to communicate. Many kinds of dolphins make whistling sounds. These sounds can help them find other dolphins.

Some kinds of dolphins cannot whistle. Instead, they make pulsed sounds that are like clicks.

Some researchers believe that each dolphin has a special call that is unique to them.

Echolocation

Dolphins use something called echolocation to find their way and look for food.

Echolocation is when an animal makes a clicking sound and listens for it to bounce off of objects. Dolphins use that echo to know where things are.

Echolocation helps dolphins when it is too dark for them to see very well.

Movement

Dolphins have bodies that are built for speed. Their shape and powerful tails allow them to swim up to 21 miles per hour.

They often swim in the **wake** of boats. They may do this to swim fast without using as much energy. They also like to play in the waves.

Dolphins are often seen breaching. They leap out of the water and land on their back, side, or belly.

21

Dolphin Calves

Dolphins usually have one baby, or calf. When they are first born, calves have to be brought to the surface so that they can breathe.

Calves are born darker in color than their parents. Their skin lightens over time.

Dolphin calves are usually ready to start hunting by the time they are two years old.

Pod Life

Dolphins are very social animals. They live in groups that are called pods. Pods are usually made up of between three and twenty dolphins.

Pods hunt, travel, play, and take care of calves together.

Pods may come together to form larger groups when they are **migrating** to warmer waters.

Lifespan

Dolphins have a long lifespan. The bottlenose dolphin, which is one of the most common dolphins, can live up to fifty years.

Many dolphins live about twenty years in the wild. They may live longer in **captivity**.

Dolphins that live in captivity are safe from fishing nets and **predators.**

Population

Many kinds of dolphins have **declining** populations. Many could be **endangered** soon and others are close to **extinction**.

Many dolphins are accidently caught in fishing nets and lines each year.

Rising temperatures are causing dolphins to go into colder waters to find food. They may have trouble **adapting** to these colder habitats.

Theme Parks

Dolphins are popular **attractions** at some theme parks and aquariums.

Some people think that dolphins should not be kept at aquariums or parks. They believe that dolphins should only be in the wild.

Dolphins that are at theme parks or aquariums may perform in shows.

Helping Dolphins

Many people are trying to help dolphins in the wild.

In the United States, the Marine Mammal Protection Act helps to protect dolphins and other mammals. It keeps people from feeding, catching, and bothering dolphins in the wild.

People have started fishing in ways that don't catch dolphins. The "Dolphin Safe" label is used on cans of tuna to show that it was caught without harming dolphins.

Researchers study dolphins so they can learn more about them. They want to learn about dolphins so they can help them.

Glossary

Adapt: to change, to adjust

Attraction: something that people want to come see

Carnivore: an animal that eats only meat

Captivity: animals that are kept by humans, not in the wild

Coast: the area where land meets the ocean

Crustacean: animals with hard, jointed shells such as crabs or shrimps.

Declining: getting smaller

Endangered: at risk of becoming

extinct

Extinct: when there are no more of

an animal left in the wild

Migrate: when animals move from

one area to another, usually

because of temperature or food

Predator: an animal that hunts other

animals for food

Wake: the waves that are created

when boats travel on the water

About the Author

Victoria Blakemore is a first grade

teacher in Southwest Florida with a

passion for reading.

You can visit her at

www.enchantedinelementary.com

Also in This Series

CPSIA information can be obtained
at www.ICGtesting.com
Printed in the USA
LVOW06*1547241117
557328LV00023B/359/P

9 781947 439436